Marvellous Maddie

Written by Kerrie Shanahan

Illustrated by Kim Woolley

Flying Start
to Literacy®

Contents

Prologue

Mr Parker, the school principal, tapped the microphone . . . tap, tap, tap. The students of Middleton Primary School had gathered for the end–of–year awards assembly.

"Thank you, everyone," said Mr Parker. "I would like to introduce our very special guest speaker, Madeline Miller. Madeline was a student at our school over thirty years ago. Since then, she has become one of our country's most successful and famous scientist. She has worked on projects that use wind power to make electricity, which has helped many, many people throughout the world.

"Here she is – Madeline Miller."

"Thank you, Mr Parker," replied Madeline.
"It's great to be back at Middleton.
I would like to begin by telling you all a
story. A story about a girl named Maddie . . ."

*   *   *   *   *

Chapter 1
Maddie's muddles

Maddie had always been curious. As a child, she loved taking things apart and tinkering. She would take apart clocks, toasters, radios, old phones, broken toys and discarded bikes.

"Mmmm," she would say. "I wonder how this works?"

At markets and garage sales, Maddie loved rummaging through the stalls. She and her grandpa would spend hours looking for useful bits and pieces and odds and ends to take apart and make into something new.

"That's marvellous, Maddie," her grandpa said each time she found a new treasure.

Maddie spent hours in Grandpa's shed. That was where she tinkered, investigated, planned, designed, invented and built.

And whenever Maddie came up with a new design, a new gadget or an invention, Grandpa would always say, "That's marvellous, Maddie!"

But Maddie's hobby wasn't always marvellous. Sometimes, it got her into all sorts of muddles!

There was the time Maddie found an old doorbell. Suddenly, she had an idea!

She used aluminium foil, wire, a battery and the doorbell to make an automatic buzzer for her bedroom.

Maddie carefully set up the circuit. She tested her design. As she opened the door, two pieces of aluminium foil touched to complete the circuit.

BBBBRRRZZZZZZ went the buzzer.

"Yes, it works!" Now Maddie would always know when someone was entering her bedroom.

But later that day, Maddie's dad was balancing a large pile of clean laundry when he opened Maddie's bedroom door.

BBBBRRRZZZZZZ went the buzzer.

"Ahhhhh!" went Dad.

He spun around so quickly that he fell over and broke his wrist.

"Sorry, Dad," said Maddie. "That wasn't meant to happen."

Then there was the time when Maddie was tinkering with a toy car. Suddenly, she had another idea!

"I know!" exclaimed Maddie. "I'll make a windup toy car for Baby Joe's first birthday."

Maddie planned, designed and built the windup car. She couldn't wait to give it to her little cousin.

"Look, Baby Joe," Maddie said. "This is how it works."

Maddie wound up the toy car.

She placed the car on the floor and slowly took her hand away.

Whoosh! Off it went, zigzagging here, there and everywhere!

Maddie beamed, but Baby Joe didn't beam.

His eyes grew big, his bottom lip dropped and he let out a roar.

Baby Joe howled, and howled, and howled!

"Sorry, Baby Joe," said Maddie. "That wasn't meant to happen."

Chapter 2
Maddie's mistake

But the worst mistake happened at school. It was Maddie's turn to clean out the fish tank.

"Mrs Rose," said Maddie, "can I try something new when I clean out the fish tank today? I've been working on a gadget that . . ."

"Oh no," interrupted Eric. "Not another invention!"

"I hope it's better than the can crusher and the paintbrush washer," added Henry.

Eric and Henry snickered.

"Stop it, boys!" said Mrs Rose.

She turned to Maddie. "Sure, Maddie!"

Maddie worked quietly at the back of the classroom. She carefully scooped out the fish and placed them in a small bowl filled with water. Then she set up the automatic cleaning device. She switched it on. Slowly, the scraper moved steadily up and down the tank walls.

"It works!" said Maddie.

"Look, Mrs Rose," said Maddie. "It . . ."

Maddie stopped mid-sentence. The mechanical arm holding the scraper was moving at double speed, in all directions. It was slapping the water . . . and water was going everywhere.

"Quick, Maddie!" said Mrs Rose. "Turn it off!"

As Maddie ran to turn off the device, she slipped on the wet floor and knocked over the science table. Plant experiments and pots of soil went flying through the air. And there was Maddie . . . sitting in the middle of a big, muddy puddle.

The class gathered around.

"What a great invention, Muddie," giggled Henry.

"Yeah, Muddie," said Eric. "Did it work?"

Eric and Henry snickered.

Mrs Rose turned off the fish tank cleaner.

"Sorry, Mrs Rose," said Maddie. "That wasn't meant to happen!"

Chapter 3

Maddie's misery

"Maddie, you need to clean up this mess," said Mrs Rose with a sigh. "Now, everyone else, please sign up for our elective day."

When Maddie had finally finished picking up the pots and cleaning up the mud, she went to sign up for the elective day. She was excited. Professor Miles from the university was running a science day.

But when Maddie went to write her name on the science elective, the word FULL was written in big, red letters.

"Mrs Rose," said Maddie, "the science elective is full."

"Sorry, Maddie," said Mrs Rose. "There's a place left in bike riding. You'll have to do that!"

Oh no, thought Maddie.

Maddie hated bike riding because it meant hot sun, flying bugs, sweaty hands and sore legs!

But Maddie had no choice. Each week, she went bike riding with her group. They were training for a special ride at the end of the school year along the track in French's Forest.

Maddie was dreading it!

Finally, the day of the ride arrived.

"Here comes Muddie!" snickered Henry and Eric, as Maddie climbed into the minibus.

This is going to be a long day! thought Maddie glumly as the bus headed to French's Forest.

Everyone was excited as they began the ride - everyone except Maddie. She was having trouble keeping up with the group.

As the riders went up a steep track, there was a sudden change in the weather. The sky turned black, and heavy drops of rain started to fall.

"Follow me," shouted Mrs Rose.

As Maddie desperately tried to keep up, she heard some voices behind her.

"Help! Help!"

Maddie stopped. In the distance, she saw two figures. There were Henry and Eric! They were way off the track, down in a small valley.

What are they doing down there? thought Maddie.

"Mrs Rose!" Maddie screamed. But there was no answer.

Maddie's heart froze with fear as she realised Mrs Rose and the group had kept on riding. What should she do? She pushed her worries to the back of her mind. She knew she had to help the boys!

Chapter 4
Maddie's mission

Maddie finally reached Eric and Henry. They were scared, wet and upset.

"We just thought we would explore the valley," sobbed Henry.

"Now we're lost," said Eric. "In a storm!"

"Let's wait here until the storm passes," said Maddie, taking control.

Finally, the wild storm passed.

"Let's get out of here," said Eric.

There was a loud crashing sound, as a large branch fell from a tree.

"Oh no!" said Henry. "Look."

Their bikes were crushed. The boys were terrified, but Maddie stayed calm.

"We need to stay in this one spot," she said. "Mrs Rose will come back."

But Maddie knew that Mrs Rose would have trouble finding them. They were a long way off the track and the sunlight was fading.

"Pass me your backpacks," said Maddie.

She emptied the contents of their packs into a big pile. Then she looked at the crumpled bikes.

"I've got it!" she said.

Maddie collected the batteries from Henry's transistor radio and the light globes from the bike lights. She unwrapped their sandwiches and smoothed out the aluminium foil.

In Eric's pencil case, she found paper clips, tape and scissors. And she cut open the silver padding of her lunch bag.

"Henry! Eric!" said Maddie. "Straighten these paper clips and twist them together to make a wire chain. Hurry! It'll be dark soon

Henry wiped away a tear.   Eric sniffled.

Maddie concentrated as she built the brightest light she could.

"Now," said Maddie, "I'm going to tie this high up in the tree so someone will see it – let's hope."

The boys watched as Maddie climbed up the tree and tied the light to the thick trunk. It was totally dark out.

Chapter 5
Maddie's medal

High up in the tree, Maddie took a deep breath. She joined two pieces of foil to complete the circuit and . . . light filled the dark sky!

"Yes!" cheered Eric and Henry. "It works!"

The silver padding from Maddie's lunch bag made the light globes shine bright and strong

"Now we wait for help," said Maddie.

For what seemed like forever, Maddie, Henry and Eric sat and waited.

At last, Maddie noticed something. "Look," she said.

In the distance, there was a faint light. Henry and Eric started yelling.

"Here! We're over here!"

Finally, the rescuers reached them.

"What a great light!" said one of the rescue workers. "We might not have found you without it."

"Maddie made it," said Henry.

"Yeah," said Eric. "It was all Maddie's idea."

And from that day on, Eric and Henry never laughed at Maddie and her ideas again!

The next day, there was a story in the local newspaper about the rescue of Maddie, Henry and Eric. And Maddie was awarded a medal for bravery.

"That's marvellous, Maddie," said Grandpa. "Just marvellous!"

And every year since, a medal has been awarded at Middleton Primary School, in Maddie's name. It is given to a student who shows a love of science.

Epilogue

"And Maddie," said Madeline Miller, "grew up and became a scientist. And that scientist is standing here today, hoping to inspire you all to follow your dreams. And now I am going to present this year's Madeline Miller Medal!"

A note from the author

When I was a child, I used to watch a TV show called The Curiosity Show. It was about all things science! The presenters used simple things such as paper clips, straws, empty containers, rubber bands and batteries to make things. Once they made a buzzer that went off if someone walked into a room – just like the one Maddie made. It was these memories that were the starting point for my story.

I wanted Maddie to be a strong character who didn't care what other people thought. She kept inventing, designing and making things anyway! As I was writing, I grew to like Maddie more and more, and I hope you like her, too!